Original title:
Tales of the Tiny Forest

Copyright © 2025 Creative Arts Management OÜ
All rights reserved.

Author: Dean Whitmore
ISBN HARDBACK: 978-1-80581-775-8
ISBN PAPERBACK: 978-1-80581-302-6
ISBN EBOOK: 978-1-80581-775-8

Heartbeats of the Forest Floor

The acorns dance, they roll and play,
While rabbits have a hop and sway.
A snail complains, so very slow,
"Why rush? I'm here to steal the show!"

A toad croaks jokes, so loud and clear,
The crickets laugh and drink their beer.
The mushrooms giggle, wearing caps,
While ants all line up for their naps.

The wind plays tricks, it whirls around,
Tickling leaves without a sound.
The shadows stretch and twist with glee,
In this world of whimsy, wild and free.

So join the fun, take off your shoes,
Let laughter echo, chase away blues.
With every heartbeat, life's a blast,
In this merry forest, joyful and vast.

The Sprightly Breeze's Song

A leaf took flight, it pirouettes,
While squirrels play poker with their pets.
The sun winks down, it paints the scene,
While shadows plot, a trickster's dream.

The breeze hums tunes to swaying trees,
As flowers dance, bending with ease.
Bees buzz along, a raucous choir,
In this micro world, never tire.

A frog on a log croaks a tune,
While butterflies flirt with the moon.
In this playful realm where nature thrives,
Joy leaps and bounds, and humor arrives.

So gather round, let laughter soar,
In every rustle, there's fun galore.
With tiny creatures, let's sing along,
To the sprightly breeze's jovial song.

Nature's Lullaby in Small Spaces

A plump little dandelion dreams,
While ladybugs sketch their prankster schemes.
Crickets compose, a symphony sweet,
As fireflies twinkle, their soft glow neat.

The owls wink down from high above,
Whispering secrets of nature's love.
A mouse in a hat throws a late-night bash,
While worms dig deep in their cozy stash.

The stars giggle, playing peek-a-boo,
As the moon tells tales, both old and new.
In the heart of night, laughter is found,
In the wiggles and giggles all around.

So cuddle close, in this forest snug,
The small spaces hum with a joyful hug.
Nature sings sweetly, a lullaby's charm,
Wrapping the creatures in warmth and calm.

Treasures Among the Twigs

Beneath the leaves, a world of fun,
Where acorns hide, 'neath rays of sun.
A treasure map drawn by a jolly fox,
Claiming the prize is just a paradox!

The pine cones jest, so full of glee,
While beetles march in a grand jubilee.
A spider weaves webs with a giggle and twist,
Creating designs that simply persist.

Amongst the twigs, a riddle does sprout,
As chipmunks dance and swirl about.
Each rustle and snap tells a story that's bold,
Of treasures hidden, both new and old.

So roam the paths, let curiosity ring,
In this quirky realm, there's joy to bring.
For in every tiny nook, you might stumble,
On laughter and fun, let your heart rumble.

The Unseen Symphony of the Saplings

In a grove where giggles sway,
Saplings dance and laugh all day.
A squirrel plays a tiny flute,
While bunnies tap their little hoot.

The mushrooms form a jolly band,
With flower petals, they make a stand.
A beetle twirls in grand ballet,
Cheering friends shout hip-hip-hooray!

The breeze joins in, a whiskered tune,
With leaves that clap beneath the moon.
A chorus sings from branches high,
While starlit sparks begin to fly.

So in the wood, when dusk is near,
The saplings play without a fear.
With giggles and joy, they end the night,
In this unseen symphony of light.

Glow of the Glistening Garden

In a patch where veggies sparkle bright,
Carrots dance in sheer delight.
Tomatoes giggle in the sun,
While radishes roll, oh what fun!

Butterflies wear funny hats,
And ants parade with lots of prats.
With broccoli crowns and peas in pods,
They form a troop of giggling gods.

A cucumber slips on a dew,
A squash yells out, 'That's just rude!'
They laugh and toss the summer breeze,
In a garden filled with silly tease.

So when the twilight starts to gleam,
The veggies weave a wacky dream.
In the glow where laughter blends,
A garden party never ends.

Nest Tales from the Needleleaf

In the needleleaf trees so tall,
A chatterbox of nests goes all.
A robin tells her hatchlings grand,
Of treasures hiding in the sand.

A wren plays tricks, it's quite absurd,
Hiding seeds, then laughing heard.
A squirrel drops his acorn prize,
And giggles echo through the skies.

The woodpecker drums a silly beat,
While owls whoop with feathered feet.
Their stories twist in vine and bark,
As daylight fades to evening dark.

So under needles, snug and tight,
The creatures share their tales each night.
Among the branches, laughter rings,
In nests where every critter sings.

Threads of the Twinkling Thicket

In the thicket where the fireflies glow,
Spiders weave their webs, a show.
With tinsel threads of silver bright,
They trap the giggles of the night.

A hedgehog rolls in a tangled spree,
While ferns sway and bend with glee.
A fox drops by to strut and boast,
'Who needs a dinner when we can toast?'

Bouncing bunnies join the dance,
In moonlit beams, they prance and prance.
The thicket hums with playful sound,
As laughter loops around and round.

When dawn peeks through the leafy guise,
The threads of fun begin to rise.
In morning's light, the giggles blend,
In the twinkling thicket, joy won't end.

Colors of the Canopy Dream

In a world where leaves wear hats,
A squirrel juggles acorns like a pro.
The turtles dance in little spats,
While fireflies put on quite the show.

Bouncing berries on each branch,
They giggle with the giggling breeze.
Frogs in tuxedos take a chance,
As buzzing bees hum some loud tease.

Raccoons don slippers, very bright,
They slide and trip, oh what a sight!
With every twist, they steal the night,
Colors spark like stars in flight.

A rainbow spills, oh what a scheme,
In this forest, we laugh and beam.
Bright colors swirl in every dream,
A canopy of silly theme.

Footprints on the Fern-Laden Path

Tiny feet on leaves they prance,
Where frogs might teach the art of dance.
Snails wear shades, they hold a glance,
As squirrels join in the merry chance.

Rabbits hop with bits of flair,
While hedgehogs spin, they seem unfair.
With one great leap, they fill the air,
As dandelions glow bright and rare.

Frolicking, the critters roam,
In every step, they make their home.
With giggles soft as nature's poem,
Footprints lead to a laughter dome.

Laughter echoes, we can't contain,
In this patch where joy's like rain.
Each footprint leaves a trace of gain,
On a trail where no one feels plain.

The Enchanted Understory

Underneath a leafy green,
A tightrope walk for ants on strings.
A dance-off starts, it's plain to glean,
As a peanut-shell band softly sings.

The mushrooms wave like magic wands,
While pixies zoom on candy wings.
A butterfly brings candy seedlings,
To fill the air with sugary strands.

Beetles boast their shiny shells,
As ladybugs strut in red coats.
In this world where laughter swells,
Every critter dreams, and floats.

Down below, where shadows play,
Cheerful whispers greet the day.
This understory spins in sway,
With giggles chasing gloom away.

Enigma of the Petal Pathways

Petals soft like whispered cheer,
Bouncing bunnies wear them well.
Bumblebees buzz without a fear,
They race in circles, under a spell.

Mysteries frolic, petals cross,
While wiggly worms spin rhymes anew.
The butterflies, they toss and toss,
In puddles formed by morning dew.

Caterpillars sing their tune,
Skipping lightly from flower to flower.
In this realm beneath the moon,
Wonder blooms with every hour.

Giggles float on the petal breeze,
Curious signs in colors tease.
In this path of plant-sown glee,
Every step whispers "happiness, please!"

Reflections in a Puddle's Eye

A frog in a puddle, dressed up in style,
Winks at the sky, with a dapper smile.
His suit made of lilies, a hat made of leaves,
He hops with such flair, it's hard to believe!

The fish do a dance, with a splash and a twirl,
As the frog shimmies down, with a leap and a whirl.
They giggle and gawk, in their watery fun,
While the puddle reflects, their tricks 'til they run.

A dragonfly zooms by, with a zoomy zing,
Challenging the frog, "Let's hop for a ring!"
With a flip and a flap, they take to the sky,
But the frog takes a bath, "Oh no! Not dry!"

They say with a laugh, it's just how life goes,
In reflections of joy, the silliness grows.
For when puddles are smiling, who needs a surprise?
Life's just a splash, with dear friends at the rise!

Secrets Carried on the Wind

Whispers of secrets tickle the sound,
As a squirrel plays tag with the breeze all around.
He flips and he flops, with a mischievous grin,
While the leaves gossip softly about his next win.

The wind tells a story to buzzing old bees,
Who buzz back in chorus, "Oh do what you please!"
A dance on the branches, oh what a delight,
With each twist and twirl, they float out of sight!

A chipmunk hears tales of the nut stash so fine,
"Where did it go? Was it lost in the pine?"
He patches up rumors, reforming the facts,
While the wind laughs along, providing the cracks.

So carry your secrets, let them take flight,
For giggles and whispers make everything bright.
Where laughter revives, until dusk bids adieu,
In the dance of the wind, what's old feels brand new!

Echoes of Tiny Winged Beings

In the hush of the night, with a flicker and flash,
Fairies scurry around, they are here in a dash.
With wings made of gossamer, they twirl and they spin,
"Catch us if you can!" giggles whispering din.

A moth, acting bold, joins the fluttering crew,
"You'll never keep pace, your running's all skew!"
With a tease and a tickle, they dance on a whim,
Lighting up moonbeams, on a whimsical rim.

Oh, the nimbleness quests, through shadows they flit,
As they giggle and whisper, "Is it us? Is it it?"
Chasing after stardust, through the soft velvet night,
Their echoes reverberate, a pure, jovial flight.

Let the tiny ones play, let the echoes resound,
In the night's gentle grip, as magic is found.
For in every soft murmur, and every quick chase,
Lies a world filled with laughter, enchantingly placed!

Sunbeams and Leafy Canopies

Sunbeams will dapple, with golden delight,
As squirrels play tag, in the warm morning light.
They scamper on branches, with leaps that amaze,
While shadows grow long, in the sun's cozy haze.

A curious rabbit, with ears that can flop,
Watches them bounce, then takes a quick hop.
With a grin on his face, he shimmies right in,
"Let's have ourselves fun! I'm the king of this spin!"

The leaves sway along, like hats on a dance,
While a beetle rolls by, in a top hat, by chance.
"Good day!" he declares, with a bow and a spin,
His fancy attire makes the critters all grin.

And so in the thicket, where sunbeams do play,
Life's a fanciful frolic, a giggle-filled way.
With laughter of friends and a canopy grand,
The forest is funny—take a jump, take a stand!

Stories of the Minuscule Grove

In a grove where acorns dance,
Snails hold parties, take a chance.
Mice wear suits to impress the crows,
While ants debate in tiny rows.

Bugs in sunglasses sip on dew,
Singing songs of a sky so blue.
Grasshoppers play hopscotch, it's true,
The bees sell honey from a shoe.

A squirrel juggles seeds with flair,
While worms wiggle in midair.
Frogs wear hats, thinking they rule,
In this quirky, tiny school.

Each leaf tells a joke or two,
As critters gather for a view.
At sundown, laughter fills the night,
In this small world, such pure delight.

Murmurs in the Moss

In soft green waves, stories creep,
Mossy whispers, secrets deep.
A ladybug tells tales of flight,
While crickets chirp with all their might.

Underneath the mushroom rim,
A tiny gnome begins to swim.
With acorn caps as boats afloat,
The frogs cheer him, and loudly gloat.

Snails engage in a race so slow,
Betting on who has more glow.
A hundred eyes on the grand prize,
The winner smiles with slimy eyes.

The evening brings a show so grand,
Fireflies twirl, a shining band.
Mossy giggles in the dark,
As creatures dance and make their mark.

Legends of the Lush Oasis

In an oasis with water so clear,
Hippos wear shades, sipping beer.
Parrots squawk a gossip-filled tale,
While lizards catch sun on a scale.

The turtles race on a slick, wet lane,
Wagers laid with jovial disdain.
Frogs in capes become the cheer,
As they chant and jump with no fear.

Coconuts roll in a playful clash,
While squirrels dive in with a splash.
The palm trees sway with rhythm divine,
In this haven where laughter aligns.

At dusk, the stars put on a show,
With fireflies acting as their glow.
In whispers soft, the tales unfold,
In a place where legends are bold.

Fables in the Ferns

Among ferns where shadows dance,
Mice find breadcrumbs by mere chance.
Lizards play tag, a fierce contest,
As fireflies light up the rest.

A squirrel tells stories of glee,
Of a game played amongst the trees.
Frogs sit in line, waiting for snacks,
While rabbits make jokes, getting the laughs.

Butterflies flutter, their wings on parade,
Dancing to tunes that the grass blades played.
In this world, the laughter flows free,
As critters unite in pure jubilee.

When twilight calls for the day's goodnight,
The fables linger, twinkling bright.
The forest giggles beneath the moon,
In this merry place where legends bloom.

Murmurs of the Minuscule Grove

In the tiny trees, a squirrel sneezes,
Mushrooms giggle, the grass just teases.
A ladybug winks, her friends hold tight,
As ants dance around, a comical sight.

A snail's in a race, oh what a blunder,
Trip over a leaf? It sounds like thunder!
Beetles in bow ties, all dressed with glee,
Critters in costume, oh what can it be?

The caterpillar sings nursery rhymes,
Chasing butterflies, lost track of the times.
A hedgehog juggles acorns not so well,
While a wise old owl just chuckles and tells.

Frogs play leapfrog, in jubilant cheer,
Splashing through puddles, they'd drink up the beer.
This tiny grove giggles, a whimsical world,
In every corner, sheer fun is unfurled.

The Enchanted Thicket

In the thicket of green, a mouse holds a feast,
With crumbs from the kitchen, he munches his least.
While bunnies play hopscotch in the sunshine,
A fat hedgehog rolls, shouting, 'Dear, pass the wine!'

Fireflies in bow ties put on a grand show,
Flitting and buzzing, they steal the bright glow.
A chipmunk collects shiny rocks for his bling,
While crickets hold concerts, their legs make us sing.

The raccoon wears glasses, reads tales from the past,
While the deer pranks the fox, oh what a contrast!
With giggles and grins echoing all around,
The enchanted thicket knows laughter unbound.

As night draws its curtain, the stars take their place,
A wise old tortoise declares, 'Let's pick up the pace!'
For even the night's filled with playful delight,
As shadows dance lightly, in the cool moonlight.

Shadows of the Woodland Sprite

In the shadiest spots, the sprites like to play,
Tripping on roots as they twirl and sway.
An acorn-knock knock, the jokes never cease,
While pixies tease frogs, 'Just hop here for peace!'

There's chatter of gnomes caught in a hammock,
Balancing donuts, oh what a panic!
A rabbit with glasses reads 'Carrots Monthly',
While a crow caws out, 'That sounds quite crunchy!'

Fairies make mischief, their giggles abound,
Sprinkling their sparkles, spreading joy all around.
And the shadows grow larger as sun starts to dip,
As the laughter cascades in a whimsical trip.

So let's join the sprites with our hearts full of cheer,
In this woodland of shadows, the fun's always near.
With dainty delights and mischief in air,
The woodland's a riot; it's quite a rare affair.

Echoes from the Woodland Floor

Down in the woods, there's a giggle or two,
As mushrooms play tricks on the wandering crew.
A squirrel tells tales of the seeds he has sown,
While a rabbit's caught napping, where sunflowers have grown.

A frog in a tuxedo croaks sweet serenades,
To the tune of the crickets, in their leafy glades.
Bees suit up for what they call 'Buzzing Wars',
While owls watch the fun from their lofty outdoor floors.

The fireflies bring light for the nighttime display,
Buzzing around, they enchant and sway.
A dance-off erupts as the moon starts to rise,
With laughter and music, beneath starry skies.

So listen closely, for echoes will soar,
Through the laughter of critters, all joys we adore.
In this woodland cacophony, fun never bores,
With each heartbeat of nature, joy simply restores.

Jubilant Jazz of the Juniper

In the shade of trees that dance and sway,
Crickets sing tunes that brighten the day.
A squirrel in shades, with a hat askew,
Zooms past a rabbit, who laughs, "Oh, boo!"

Breezes blow softly, tickling the leaves,
As ants march in lines, seeking juicy treats.
A grasshopper twirls, with a leap and a spin,
While owls swap gossip, all laughs and grins.

Toadstools are chairs for gnomes sipping cheer,
As pixies perform, their laughter rings clear.
The fireflies flicker, a winking parade,
While shadows play games in this joyful glade.

Under the stars, the laughter rings wide,
Each creature joins in for the nighttime ride.
With jazzy giggles and foot-tapping cheer,
The forest's a stage for the wild to appear.

Harmony of the Hidden Hues

In a patch of green where the colors collide,
Butterflies flutter, like confetti they glide.
An odd little fish with a bow tie and hat,
Tells stories of mud to a giggling cat.

The trees wear their hats made of vibrant flair,
While snails glide along with a pace none compare.
Moles play the drums with their tiny little hands,
And daisies join in, forming groovy bands.

A fox with a mustache, so suave and so sly,
Makes jokes with the owl who's too wise to cry.
In the darker corners, trolls tell tales bold,
Of friendships with bogs and adventures of old.

Together they gather, all colors and sounds,
In a festival where no square inch confounds.
Here harmony reigns, with each laugh and shout,
Hidden hues glowing, in laughter about.

Scrolls of the Sprouting Seedlings

In a pot of soil, the seedlings chat loud,
"Do you think we'll grow tall, or just make a crowd?"
Worms play the champ, as they wiggle and turn,
While wise bees recite what the flowers can learn.

The sprouts make a pact to grow big and stout,
While ants march beside them, singing about.
"Let's reach for the sky, not get lost down below,
Or we'll end up a salad," a radish says, "No!"

Sunlight brings giggles from the daisies spry,
Each bud has a secret, no one knows why.
The vines twist and tangle in radiant glee,
As roots whisper stories beneath the old tree.

Tiny yet mighty, these seeds plant their dreams,
In rainbows of color, they burst at the seams.
With scrolls full of laughter, they stretch and they sway,
Celebrating growth in their own funny way.

Whimsy Amongst the Wildflowers

In fields where the flowers do prance and sway,
Bees put on shows with their buzzing ballet.
With hats made of clover and tails made of straws,
They sip on the nectar, sharing sweet applause.

Dandelions puff, making wishes on air,
As butterflies flutter without a care.
A hedgehog in shades rolls by in a whirl,
Chasing a giggle, that's pink with a twirl.

Tall daisies gossip with their heads in a huddle,
About the young kids who explore the muddy puddle.
"Did you see that squirrel? What a silly sight!
He tried to dance, but he tripped in moonlight!"

Among petals bright, the laughter does bloom,
A patchwork of joy where no darkness can loom.
With whimsy found here, let the giggles unfurl,
Amongst the wild blooms, life's a hilarious swirl.

Shadows of the Sprightly Squirrels

In a tree with a twist, a squirrel's grand leap,
He teeters, he wobbles, he's lost in a heap.
With acorns aplenty, he starts up a dance,
While the birds in the branches just giggle and prance.

He chats with the chipmunks, they chuckle away,
A contest of speed sends them scampering gay.
With fluffy tails flying, they zoom through the air,
Yet trip on a twig, oh what a fine scare!

The shadow of trouble looms close to their path,
As the grumpy old owl lets out a loud laugh.
These whirlwinds of mischief, they scamper and shout,
With laughter and joy, they are never without!

So here's to the critters, nut-gathering fools,
In the forest from dusk till the morning bright cools.
With giggles and jumbles, they play on their way,
Ensuring each moment is filled with their play.

Glimmers in the Gossamer Glade

In a glade where light flickers, a fairy flies by,
With wings made of whispers, and laughter on high.
She tickles the flowers, and they giggle out loud,
As petals do parties, all joyous and proud.

A glow-worm, quite chubby, joins in for a jig,
He twirls 'round the daisies, getting mighty big.
With glittery sparkle, he lights up the night,
While the mushrooms all twirl in a colorful sight.

A playful old toad hops right in the fray,
He croaks silly tunes, in a musical way.
But just when they chuckle, the sun starts to peek,
And the giggles dissolve, as they all begin to sneak.

Yet memories linger in the glimmering glade,
Where laughter and fun made the evening parade.
So come back tomorrow, when the fun will repeat,
In whispers and wiggles, beneath the moon's seat.

Interludes of the Insect Kingdom

A beetle in polka-dots rolls down the lane,
With ambition so bold, and a hint of disdain.
He challenges ants to a race 'round the stone,
But the ants roll their eyes, they're busy with loan.

The butterflies giggle as they float up above,
While a buzzing old bee is in search of some love.
With plucky confessions and pollen in hand,
He stumbles and fumbles; oh, isn't love grand?

The crickets are crooning their late-night serenade,
As ladybugs tango, a fun little parade.
But suddenly startled, they all take to flight,
At the sight of a frog with intentions not right!

Yet joy fills the air as they dance through the grass,
In the kingdom of insects, where moments amass.
With laughter and flutter, they live without fear,
In this bustling bazaar, where friendship is near.

Verses of the Verdant Veil

Amidst buzzing thickets, a green sprite arrives,
With a grin on her face, she plans grand high-fives.
She measures the leaves for a game of hide-and-seek,
While the worms roll their eyes, bored and quite meek.

A hedgehog, all prickly, joins in for some fun,
With a plan to surprise, not to be outdone.
He tucks in his grains and curls up with glee,
To scare all his friends, oh, how clever is he!

The vines sway and shimmy, as the thicket hums,
While the sprite leads her pals, oh, the giggling numbs!
But the laughter grows louder as night starts to fall,
The critters collide in a joyous free-for-all!

So here in the cover, beneath leafy embrace,
Friendship is woven, like sunbeams they chase.
In verses of frolic, the forest ignites,
With silly adventures that last through the nights.

Whispers Among the Moss

In a nook where critters play,
A snail sings loud, in its own way.
With laughter shared beneath the trees,
A hedgehog dances with the bees.

The mushrooms giggle in a row,
As tiny ants put on a show.
They boast the bravest, fiercest tales,
Of windswept stumps and boyish snails.

A squirrel winks and scampers high,
While frogs debate the clouds and sky.
In shadows where the shadows laugh,
A chipmunk plots a daring path.

And so they frolic, hand in hand,
In whispers soft, both sweet and grand.
In mossy beds beneath the sun,
The tiny forest's never done.

Beneath the Canopy's Embrace

Beneath the boughs where stories spin,
A fox in boots begins to grin.
With acorns tossed like little darts,
The forest holds its giggling hearts.

A raccoon jests, a shifty thief,
Stealing snacks—Oh, what a relief!
Each veggie he's snatched, a juicy jest,
A pickled peach for his great feast.

Two owls hoot their secret code,
While ladybugs parade their road.
A beetle bounces, claiming he's,
The king of all that sways in breeze.

Where shadows dance and giggles soar,
In leafy realms, forever more.
Each creature finds their perfect place,
Beneath the canopy's warm embrace.

Secrets of the Sylvan Space

In hidden nooks where whispers play,
A wise old owl leads the way.
Through tangled roots, with laughter bold,
A story spins, a joy to hold.

The caterpillars shimmy and sway,
In secret meetings, plotting their day.
With wings in dreams, they glide and glide,
As fireflies join the joyful ride.

A mossy turtle, oh how he brags,
And shares his tales of playful jags.
With each retelling, giggles grow,
In secret glades where few may go.

The magic brews, a funny sight,
As beetles waltz into the night.
In sylvan spaces, full of grace,
The forest thrives in its funny chase.

Chronicles of the Little Green

In patches bright of little green,
So much mischief can be seen.
A grasshopper hops, and what a leap,
While ladybugs quietly peep.

The laughter bubbles, a wooded song,
As tiny tales seem to prolong.
A mouse wears stripes, a dashing trend,
Each twig a stage for the forest's end.

Chirping crickets form a band,
With thistle leaves as their grand stand.
While ants parade in perfect lines,
A circus showing, purest signs.

With every nook, a story blooms,
In creaky beds where magic looms.
Chronicles shared with joyful flair,
In Little Green, no worries there.

Adventures of the Hidden Hollow

In a hollow tree where critters play,
A squirrel lost his hat on a dewy day.
The rabbit laughed as he took a hop,
While the owl wondered if it was a prop.

The fox wore a coat that was slightly too tight,
Trying to dance under the moonlight bright.
The raccoon rolled in leaves, what a sight!
As the badger snored on, dreaming of flight.

A tiny bridge made of twigs and glue,
Was crossed by a snail, oh what a view!
The bugs cheered on, waving tiny flags,
While a ladybug giggled, holding her jags.

At sunset, they gathered in laughter and cheer,
With stories so silly, for all to hear.
In the hidden hollow, fun never ends,
As nature's own comedies twist and blend.

Chronicles of the Woodland Spirits

The woodland spirits, full of cheer,
Played hide and seek throughout the year.
One peeked out from behind a tree,
While another climbed high, full of glee.

A sprite juggled acorns on a log,
As a gnome told tales of a dancing frog.
The laughter echoed through leafy trails,
While a mouse in a vest recounted his sails.

They sipped on dew from morning's first light,
And danced with shadows that skipped out of sight.
With mischief in heart, they spun a grand tale,
Of the squirrel who thought he could ride a whale!

When dusk painted skies with colors so bright,
They promised to meet with the next morning's light.
In the woods, where wonders swirl and play,
Their cheerful spirits never fade away.

Life Beneath the Bark

Beneath the bark, where the roly-poly beds,
A wiggly worm shops for some leafy threads.
He found a cap that was way too big,
And danced around like an excitable pig.

A beetle wore glasses, quite posh and neat,
While the ants marched in line, with their tiny feat.
They laughed at the worm, who tripped with style,
Creating a ruckus that spread for a mile.

The woodpecker tapped out a silly tune,
As the mushrooms swayed under the glowing moon.
A dance-off began among creatures so spry,
With the grasshoppers leaping to reach the sky.

As night whispered softly, they snuggled in tight,
Under the stars, they giggled 'til light.
In life beneath bark, where oddities roam,
Every raucous moment felt just like home.

Dreams of the Diminutive Dell

In a dell so small, where the daisies bloom,
Lived a tiny frog who fancied a broom.
He swept all day, making flowers laugh,
As bumblebees buzzed, sharing their path.

The ants held a party, with cupcakes galore,
While a mouse in a tie knocked at the door.
"Come join us!" he squeaked, with crumbs on his chin,
As they feasted on treats, letting giggles spin.

A butterfly swooped in, wearing a hat,
The frog gleamed bright, "What is this? Fancy that!"
With a whirl and a twirl, she took to the air,
Creating a whirlwind of laughter and flair.

As twilight descended, they danced on the grass,
With shadows twirling, they let the night pass.
In the dell so small, dreams took flight,
Where hilarity blossomed under the moonlight.

Melodies of the Murmuring Brooks

A frog with a hat, sings tunes so grand,
While fish throw a party, at his command.
The crickets are drumming, the ants do the dance,
A wild, wacky bash, if given a chance.

The water's a stage, the reeds wave along,
As turtles in bow ties serenade with a song.
One fish does a jig, splashing all about,
While frogs crack up, with a ribbiting shout.

A bubbling brook's laughter tickles the day,
With snickers and giggles that float and sway.
The sun comes to join, gives a wink and a spin,
As nature's sweet choir breaks out in a grin.

So if you feel low, head to the stream,
Where humor abounds, and all critters beam.
They'll show you their world of hilarious sights,
And leave you in stitches, on breezy, bright nights.

Echoing Laughter of the Little Ones

The little ones wander, with giggles that ring,
In mushroom-top hats, they do silly things.
With ladybugs laughing, they leap, hop, and bound,
Turning flowers to trumpets, sweet music around.

A squirrel in a wig, with a nutty ballet,
Dances under the sun, come join in the play!
While owls look confused, they hoot 'What's the fuss?'
As rabbits get wild, and jump on the bus.

There's a race through the grass, with beetles in tow,
While hedgehogs in polka dots steal the show.
The trees bend with laughter, the breeze swirls the cheer,
As fireflies twinkle, saying, "Come here!"

At dusk, when they settle, they dream of the chase,
With whispers of giggles that'll brighten your face.
In moments of joy, you'll not wanna depart,
For the world of the tiny, is a mirror to the heart.

Twilight Whispers of the Treetops

As twilight descends, the branches do sway,
Whispering secrets, of fun through the day.
With owls telling jokes, that make the stars snicker,
The sunset's a canvas, with colors that flicker.

A raccoon in pajamas, so cozy and bright,
Dines on sweet berries, all while taking flight.
As squirrels throw acorns, like confetti so fine,
Then giggle and shout, "Hey, it's party time!"

The shadows grow long, and whispers grow bold,
Tales of mischief, in hues of pink and gold.
With crickets as the chorus, they sing with delight,
A twilight of laughter, into the night.

So join in the mirth, in the trees up so high,
Where the tiniest creatures laugh under the sky.
In whispers of joy, they spin the moon's thread,
And the world before you, turns giggles instead.

Secrets of the Sylvan Sanctuary

In a realm where the giggles and sunshine meet,
The trees share secrets, oh, what a treat!
With mushrooms as pillows, and twigs as a stage,
The critters perform, in a forest rampage.

The chipmunks are jesters, with tricks up their sleeves,
While owls lift their brows, astonished at thieves.
A sly fox in spectacles, reads from a book,
Of cookies and capers, with a mischievous look.

The bees throw confetti, of sweet golden light,
And butterflies giggle, with colors so bright.
Each whisper they share, is a giggle unfurled,
In this secret haven, of a funny, warm world.

With echoes of laughter, this sanctuary flows,
Through roots and through branches, where pure joy grows.
So come join the fun, in this woodland parade,
For the secrets of laughter, will surely not fade.

Legends of the Secret Understory

In the soil where the worms like to dance,
A tiny squirrel prances, lost in his trance.
He thinks he's a knight, with a leaf for a shield,
Battling ants in a brave little field.

A mushroom, like a castle, stands tall and proud,
With snails as the guards and a ladybug crowd.
They sip dewdrop tea, gossiping 'til noon,
About the great worm that whistled a tune.

The beetles hold court on a twig that they claim,
Declaring their kingdom, the Bugle Bug fame.
Each laugh echoes loud through the roots and the vines,
As the spiders spin stories in silken designs.

Under leaves where the sunlight just barely leaks,
The faeries do yoga, with wiggly tweaks.
They giggle and tumble, all nimble and spry,
Before taking a nap on a sweet butter pie.

Mysteries of the Miniature Wild

In the wild where the tiniest creatures convene,
A grasshopper juggles with acorns so green.
The ants march in line, with plans to explore,
But they all end up lost—who could ask for more?

There's a caterpillar who dreams of a race,
But it takes so much time to grow legs with grace.
His friends cheer him on from the soft, dewy grass,
While he teaches a snail how to run—a bold class.

A hedgehog once tried to fly high in the sky,
With balloons made of dandelions, oh so shy!
He floated then plummeted, landing with charms,
On a patch of soft clovers, safe from all harms.

And when day turns to dusk, in the soft, winding trails,
The crickets give concerts, while the owl tells tales.
In this world of small wonders, big laughs take their place,

As every tiny creature finds joy in the race.

Flickers of Light in the Green Depths

In a thicket so thick where the glowworms glow,
A firefly spent his last dime on a show.
With lights all aglow, he danced 'round with glee,
While a frog croaked the beat, who loved jazz by the sea.

Beneath wrinkled roots, there's a party we hear,
With shrooms on the table, and laughter is near.
The beetles tap dance, while the spiders spin low,
Creating a rhythm that steals every show.

A chipmunk with dreams of a grand Broadway play,
Wrote a script for a show, but then lost his way.
He acted alone, with a seed as his muse,
But forgot all the lines—what a terrible ruse!

Yet still under stars, where the night breezes weave,
Joy echoes through leaves, as each creature believes.
In this laughter-filled world of dimming daylight,
All dare to be silly, in flickering light.

Mycelium Dreams and Fern Wishes

In the soil where the mushrooms weave dreams in the night,
A snail holds a wish that he'd fly like a kite.
His friends all just chuckle and say, 'Not a chance!
But we can all dream, so come join us, let's prance!'

What happens when ferns start to whisper and sigh?
All the squirrels lean in, asking 'What's up in the sky?'
The ferns giggle softly, they know all the lore,
Of the frogs and their tales from the bank of the shore.

There's a hedgehog who wears all the mushrooms he finds,
Decked out like a prince in the woodland designs.
He tells silly jokes as he wobbles around,
While the others all laugh at his spiky crown.

And when starlight blankets the forest so wide,
Fanciful wishes take root and abide.
In this joy-filled domain, we all dance and play,
Where mycelium schemes spark adventures each day.

Indigos in the Iridescent Inlet

In a swirl of blue by the shore,
A fish donned a hat, wanted more.
He danced with glee, gave a tug,
To a crab in a coat, snug as a bug.

They laughed as the tide rolled in like a crew,
While seagulls squawked, 'What are you two?'
The fish flipped a fin and stole the show,
With jellybean friends in a shimmering row.

But a wave took the hat, oh what a steal!
The crab said, 'Don't worry, I'll wear its appeal!'
Together they splashed with hilarious leaps,
In the inlet, where the laughter keeps.

So, if you venture along that bright bay,
Keep an eye out for fish, fancy and gay.
They might just unite, for a whimsical spree,
With a crab in a coat, singing out with glee.

Nestled Narratives of the Nature's Bounty

In the shadows, the squirrels share,
Nutty secrets with flair,
They giggle and plot, while they munch on seeds,
Trading acorns like treasure, fulfilling their needs.

One claims a stash of a ghostly nut,
Swearing it's special, in a hidden hut.
The others erupt in a fit of delight,
Imagining fireflies dancing at night.

Then a hedgehog with spectacles stepped in,
To share tales of rabbits, quite the win.
Fables of cakes baked beneath leafy crowns,
Had all of them rolling, bumping their frowns.

As twilight arrived, the laughter grew loud,
With the forest their stage, they felt quite proud.
Nestled tales, spun under moonlight's glow,
In this quirky, wild world, let the antics flow.

Portraits from the Petiole Path

On the pathway lined with shimmering greens,
A dapper snail donned just the right sheen.
He posed with flair on a frond made of lace,
While following behind, a clumsy raccoon in a race.

The raccoon tumbled, flipping his hat,
His arms flailing wildly, like a goofy acrobat.
'Oh dear! Watch your step!' the snail gave a shout,
'You're painting the path, there's no need to pout!'

Along came a millipede, all decked in beads,
He twirled and he whirled, fulfilling their needs.
'Throw a snack party! Come one, come all!'
With loop-de-loops, they answered the call.

Each twist and turn brought laughter so sweet,
Creating portraits where giggles compete.
Beneath leafy boughs, where the antics took form,
Life's whimsical brush strokes began to swarm.

Gossamer Dreams on Damp Ferns

Upon soft greens where the dew beads cling,
A frog in a cape, began to sing.
His voice was a croak, laced with delight,
As fireflies twinkled, lighting the night.

With whispers of wishes, the ferns proudly sway,
A moth in a tutu joined the ballet.
They leapt through the air, like stars on a spree,
Chasing shadows in harmony, wild and free.

Then a snail joined in, playing tambourine,
Beats made of rain drops, a joyful sheen.
Together they danced, each step a cheer,
In gossamer dreams, where friends disappear.

So, if you wander where damp ferns bloom,
Look for the party that bursts into zoom.
With laughter and rhythms, they're sure to enthrall,
In the heart of the forest, there's fun for us all.

Guardians of the Tiny Glades

In the glades where critters prance,
The squirrel wears a tiny pants.
The rabbit giggles at the show,
As flowers dance, and breezes blow.

A hedgehog dons a crown so bright,
Declaring himself the king of night.
With acorn scepters, they decree,
All snacks are shared in harmony.

A dance-off 'neath the silver moon,
Where fireflies flicker, piper's tune.
The wise old owl insists on grace,
But ends up tripping on a face.

And all the woodland critters laugh,
At guardians' silly photograph.
With leafy hats and leafy ties,
They pose beneath the starry skies.

Journey Through the Shrubbery

Two ants in hats set forth to roam,
One claims he's far from home sweet home.
They tumble through the thicket wide,
In search of snacks, with silly pride.

A bushy brow on a grumpy fox,
He shouts, 'Get off my garden rocks!'
But ants convinced he's only jest,
Share crumbs of bread, which he loves best.

They meet a ladybug who sings,
And twirls about on dainty wings.
They dance in circles, what a spree,
The garden knows such jubilee!

With giggles echoing everywhere,
Tiny friends with hearts to share.
As twilight paints the sky so bright,
They trek back home, with hearts alight.

The Sparkling Dew's Journey

A drop of dew, so round and clear,
Decides to roll without a fear.
It tumbles down a silky leaf,
Then lands near ants, who sigh in grief.

They're scheming hard to take a sip,
But dew has plans; it takes a trip.
It bounces past the morning sun,
Where dandelions start to run.

"Oh no," they say, "they're spry indeed!"
While dew just giggles, full of speed.
It races raindrops, drips with glee,
In every splash, it shouts, "Whee!"

The journey ends on a petal bright,
Where tiny friends cheer with delight.
A sparkling crown for such a run,
In dew's adventures, there's so much fun!

Whimsy in the Woodland Shadows

In shadows deep where whispers play,
A mouse spins yarns of night and day.
With cheese to share and giggles loud,
    He entertains the forest crowd.

A hedgehog rolls in apple skin,
    Declaring, "I've a new found twin!"
While bunnies leap and tickle toes,
Through leafy archways, laughter flows.

A silly frog with floppy eyes,
    Tries to fly, but only sighs.
He jumps and trips on mushrooms wide,
The woodland echoes with their pride.

The fireflies join to light the way,
As friends share stories come what may.
In woodland shadows, joy's abound,
    With whimsy sprouting all around.

Puffballs and Periwinkles

In a patch of soft green grass,
Puffballs dance with gentle sass.
They tickle toes and tease the breeze,
While periwinkles giggle with ease.

A mushroom cap donned like a hat,
Befriends a snail—oh, imagine that!
They plot a scheme to steal some pie,
As ants march past, they dream and sigh.

The days roll on with silly games,
With clouds above calling their names.
They leap for joy, they stumble too,
In laughter's grip, they make a zoo.

At twilight's end, they share a cheer,
Awaiting stars that soon appear.
With every puff and wink they share,
The forest hums, a lively air.

Mirth of the Moths

Under moonlight, moths take flight,
Twirling 'round in sheer delight.
With laughter soft like evening air,
They flutter with a carefree flair.

They wear cloaks of shimmering dust,
And dance on petals, oh, how they trust!
A silly game of hide and seek,
Each giggle soft and mildly sneak.

A firefly joins the twisty fun,
Their glow could outshine the morning sun.
With every flap, a chuckle's born,
As shadows stretch into the morn.

In whispers shared, they plot and plan,
To host a party—oh, what a jam!
Their nightly frolics weave a tale,
Of wings and laughter, where dreams set sail.

Cryptic Chronicles of Twilight

In twilight's hush, secrets are spun,
As critters gather for some fun.
A hedgehog tells of roundabout,
His tales of mischief fill with clout.

The shadows giggle, the stars peek in,
As raccoons chime with a cheeky grin.
A slippery tale of thievery shared,
Leaves all in stitches, none are scared.

A wily fox sketches out a plan,
For a heist so bold, it's quite the scam!
But tripping over his own big tail,
He tumbles down, his scheme's a fail.

Yet laughter echoes through the night,
As every creature shares delight.
These chronicles, cryptic yet bright,
Bring joy and fun till morning light.

Swinging Stories from the Sycamores

In sycamores, where squirrels play,
They swing on branches, make their way.
Each jump gives birth to silly tales,
Of acorn treasures and misfit whales.

A parrot squawks about a race,
But tripping over, loses grace!
Dizzy and dazed, he tells a joke,
While all around begin to choke.

From cozy nooks to leafy heights,
They forge their stories by the lights.
Their laughter ripples through the boughs,
As every creature takes a bow.

At dusk they gather, tales to share,
Under stars, without a care.
With swinging hearts, they celebrate,
In sycamores, they revel—great!

Requiem of the Rustling Leaves

In a whispering dance, they chat and they sway,
"Why don't the branches come out to play?"
A chattering squirrel drops acorns with glee,
"Oops! I meant to save them for my afternoon tea!"

The fox in a jacket, looking quite dapper,
Steals a glance at the moon, now that's quite a caper!
"Is it dinner time? I'm starving!" he's bold,
As shadows don costumes of silver and gold.

In a puddle, a frog finds his throne on a leaf,
Pretending he's king, if only for brief.
He croaks loud announcements, applauds his own show,
All the forest critters gather 'round for the fro!

As night settles softly, they giggle and cheer,
The mischief has woven a tapestry here.
With rustling leaves, they dream of the day,
When all will unite in this woodland ballet.

Fir-Scented Fantasies

In the heart of the grove, the branches align,
To weave silly stories of how they all dine.
"Last week, the oak tried to dance with a bee,
But that bee's not a partner, just buzzing with glee!"

A hedgehog in spectacles reads poetry near,
While chipmunks recite with a tremor of cheer.
"Is poetry like cheese? Or is it like wine?"
"It's better with crackers! Now pass me the brine!"

Beneath the tall firs, a party takes shape,
With toads in tuxedos and ferns in a cape.
They twirl through the night, as the stars blink and wink,
And ponder deep questions, like "Do frogs really stink?"

From high above, a wise owl takes flight,
"Who's stealing my hoot? I need answers tonight!"
With laughter and jokes, they share every jest,
In this enchanted grove, they giggle their best.

Blush of the Blossoming Buds

The flowers all whispered, "We're shy of our hues!"
The daisies looked bashful, the violets blues.
So they spun a tale of who'd bloom the best,
With laughter and petals, they put it to test!

The tulips took bets, each bloom brimming bold,
"I'll outshine the sun, just watch me unfold!"
While bumblebees buzzed, confused by the fuss,
"We're not here for drama, just flowers and us!"

A beetle with shades strutted right down the lane,
"Look at me sparkle! I'm totally vain!"
As blooms giggled softly, and trees rolled their trees,
A lilac retorted, "Oh please! Not the bees!"

In a riot of colors, they painted the air,
With giggles and grins, without any care.
As blossoms united, a mischievous kin,
They painted the garden with cheeky, bright grin!

Awakening the Wishful Woods

A hedgehog in dreams found a magical gate,
Where wishes were granted, though never quite straight.
"I'll wish for a castle, a crown on my head!"
But a squirrel just snickered, "You're better off fed!"

There's a flirting fern trying to show off its flair,
With a shake of its fronds and a twirl in the air.
"Won't you join me, dear beetle? We'll dance in the sun!"

But the beetle replied, "You dance? That's just fun!"

As a woodpecker drummed on a tree with a laugh,
"Your dreams are so silly, I'm splitting my calf!"
A bouquet of mushrooms chortled in cheer,
"Let's dream up a feast! Who wants fruit? Come here!"

With laughter and whimsy, the woods came to life,
As critters and fungi forgot all their strife.
They twirled in the moonlight, till dawn showed its face,
In a wishful woods gala, where silliness lives!

Adventures in the Leafy Sanctuary

In the shady grove, the ants have a race,
Laughing and tumbling, they pick up the pace.
A snail on a skateboard joins in the spree,
Wheeling around like a leaf-blown decree.

A squirrel on stilts, oh what a delight,
Trying to juggle acorns, a comical sight.
The flowers all giggle, petals all shake,
As the playful pranksters plan their next break.

A hedgehog with glasses reads jokes out loud,
The mushrooms are chuckling, a chuckling crowd.
They dance in the breeze, on their little toes,
While the wind whispers softly, and everyone knows.

With creatures so tiny, mischief they weave,
Each day is a romp, it's hard to believe.
Bright mushrooms in hand, they flaunt their bold style,
In the leafy sanctuary, laughter's worthwhile.

Stories from the Woodland Nook

In a nook by the creek, the critters convene,
With stories of legends, both silly and keen.
A frog in a crown claims he's king of the lane,
While the dragonflies giggle, oh what a reign!

A wise old owl hoots from his perch high above,
Claiming he's the reason for every "tree love."
The mice bring the cheese, they toast with delight,
To the tales spun beneath the moonlight so bright.

In a circle of friends, the raccoon reveals,
How he once won a race on his trusty old wheels.
A bushy-tailed squirrel just snorts with a grin,
"No one can outrun me, let the fun begin!"

A beetle with spectacles tells of his quests,
Of dodging a shoe and unreliable guests.
As laughter erupts, the night carries on,
In the woodland nook, like a whimsical song.

The Hidden Realm of Petals

In a garden of wonder, each petal's a shade,
A bee with a top hat is often waylaid.
He talks to a toad who's lost in a dream,
"Should I buzz or should I hop?" - it's silliness supreme!

A butterfly ballerina twirls with flair,
While the daisies applaud, tossing pollen in air.
A mischievous ladybug plans a surprise,
Poking fun at the snails, with laughter in their eyes.

As the sun shines down, with a jubilant glow,
A worm joins the dance, oh what a show!
With petals as plates, they feast on sweet dew,
Each moment a banquet – who knew life was true?

In this hidden realm, where giggles ignite,
Nature's own jesters keep spirits so bright.
So when you walk by, take a moment to pause,
For laughter awaits, just because!

Dance of the Diminutive Creatures

Under the moonlight, a grand dance is held,
With fireflies buzzing, their glow brightly spelled.
A tiny toad in a tuxedo so slick,
Shimmies and shakes with an entertaining trick.

Whiskered and giggling, the mice spin around,
In tiny top hats, their eight-legged sound.
A hedgehog on bass, with acorns for drums,
Keeps the beat steady, while joyfulness hums.

A grasshopper leaps, ballet-like, through air,
A carousel dancer, full of style, and flair.
Dandelions twirl, holding hands in a ring,
All creatures united, their hearts full of spring.

With mushrooms for seats, they rest and exchange,
Silly little stories—they're never too strange.
In the dance of the small, laughter is key,
In a world so vast, they're happy and free.

Echoes of the Honeyed Glade

In the glade where bees play hide and seek,
A squirrel lost his acorn, oh so bleak.
The flowers laugh and start to sway,
While butterflies tease, 'Come join our fray!'

A frog wearing glasses took a leap,
He tripped on a snail who was fast asleep.
With a ribbit and a tumble, they both swirled,
Creating chaos in this sweet, tiny world.

A ladybug donned a little crown,
Chasing her subjects who dashed around.
'Catch me if you can,' she giggled loud,
As the ants all marched, feeling quite proud.

Just when the sun began to set bright,
The critters gathered for a dance that night.
They waltzed on petals, twirled with glee,
In the honeyed glade, oh what a spree!

Chronicles from the Underbrush

In the underbrush, where mischief thrives,
A hedgehog dreams of wild, silly dives.
He zigged and zagged, all in a spin,
Bouncing off mushrooms, oh, what a win!

A group of beetles wore hats askew,
Debating if rain could taste like dew.
A snail chimed in with a wiggly chat,
'The slower, the better, that's where it's at!'

A curious mole peeked up through the soil,
'Why do you dance when you could just toil?'
But the others just giggled, a merry crew,
Exploring the world, with a point of view.

In the twilight glow, stories were spun,
Of hops and skips, oh, what fun was done!
With every chuckle, their hearts felt light,
In the underbrush, where joy took flight.

Dances Among the Daisies

Where daisies bloom and butterflies flit,
A chipmunk shows off his latest skit.
He twirled in circles, then leaped so high,
'Is that a dance or just a silly try?'

Nearby, a badger with a top hat wide,
Joined in the fun with a rambunctious stride.
'I'll show you moves that will make you grin,'
And with that, he slipped but turned it to win.

The caterpillars rolled, sparking delight,
'We may be small, but we dance all night!'
A chorus of chuckles filled the warm air,
As laughter united each creature there.

As the moonlight danced on the petals' white,
They boogied and wiggled, all through the night.
In this garden where mirth takes the lead,
Among the daisies, joy is the seed!

Reveries of the Leafy Realm

In the leafy realm, where whispers play,
A raccoon juggled with nuts in dismay.
His paws flew wild in a flurry of cheer,
As the squirrels all cheered, 'You're the star here!'

An owl wore spectacles, wise and round,
Declared a contest, the best sound around.
The mice all squeaked with a rhythm so neat,
While a turtle tapped slowly, keeping the beat.

The wind chimed in with a rustle and laugh,
As the ants formed a conga line path.
With giggles and wiggles, they shuffled and spun,
In the leafy delight, all hearts were won.

When shadows grew long, they gathered to share,
Their funniest moments, free of all care.
With joy in their hearts, and gleams in their eyes,
In the leafy realm, their laughter would rise!

Serenade of the Starlit Silence

In a darkened wood, frogs croak with glee,
Singing to crickets, a chorus so free.
The owl hoots loudly, 'What's all this noise?'
But the raccoons dance, those mischievous boys!

A firefly twirls, wearing a bright hat,
While a squirrel chuckles, 'What do you think of that?'
The trees sway gently, they join in the fun,
Under the soft glow of the moon and the sun.

With whispers of breeze, the night puts on show,
Every rustle and cackle, a magical flow.
A snail on a leaf keeps time with a beat,
Declaring a concert that's wild and complete!

In this starlit silence, joy finds its way,
Where laughter is boundless and night turns to day.
As nature's own orchestra plays with delight,
The woodlands rejoice in the moon's silver light.

Celebrations at the Creek's Edge

A party is brewing down by the stream,
Where dragonflies flutter and sunbeams gleam.
The fish leap with joy, splashing with cheer,
While frogs raise their glasses: 'A toast, let's make clear!'

With cupcakes of daisies, a feast on the way,
The ants hoof it over, they dance and they sway.
'Who ordered the pies?' squeaks a mouse in confusion,
But no one will budge from the mishap's illusion.

The toad sings a tune that's catchy and loud,
While the rabbits hop 'round, ecstatic and proud.
The raccoons bring snacks made of acorns and nuts,
It's pure comedy seeing their silly little cuts!

As twilight arrives with a splash of orange,
All creatures rejoice in this colorful barrage.
The creek bubbles laughter, a bubbly delight,
In a gathering filled with pure joy through the night!

Riddles from the Rustling Reeds

In the thicket so green, whispers take flight,
As reeds tell their stories in the soft twilight.
'What has a tail but never can run?'
A wily old turtle just grins, 'Oh, what fun!'

The field mice giggle, their tails in a twist,
When asked 'Hey, what's something you really can't miss?'
'The glittering stars!' squeaks one with a quake,
While they snatch at the shadows, giggling, not fake.

An otter chimes in with a whimsy-filled tease,
'What makes a sound but not air in the trees?'
'Your question's absurd!' the wise hedgehog retorts,
Much to the chagrin of some fun-seeking cohorts.

Through rustling reeds, riddles echo, they say,
With chuckles and snickers, they brighten the day.
Each answer a treasure, absurdity reigns,
In this lively realm where laughter never wanes.

Breeze of the Blushing Blossoms

Petals parade, flaunting colors galore,
A breeze tickles daisies, they giggle and soar.
A butterfly flutters, 'I believe I will stay!'
While a woodpecker shouts, 'Hey, watch my ballet!'

The blooms hold a meeting, discussing their hues,
'Who wore it best?' they declare with a fuse.
A tulip quips, 'Red's nice, but I'm quite the show!'
While sunflowers nod, proud, all in a row.

A dandelion whispers, 'Let's float our own way!'
And puffs send their wishes, come out to play.
They twirl in the wind, toss their seeds with delight,
Making tiny wishes take off into the night.

Oh, what joy in the breeze, amongst petals so bright,
Each flower still laughing, beneath stars so light.
With petals a-dance, and laughter that swells,
In this garden of whimsy, there's magic that dwells!

Insights from the Enchanted Grove

In a grove so bright and green,
The mushrooms danced, a lively scene.
A squirrel in shades, quite the sight,
Declared himself the fashion knight.

The wise old owl, with glasses perched,
Said, "Wisdom's not just for the searched!"
A crow cawed back, quite out of tune,
"Just don't ask me to sing a croon!"

A froggy band played on a log,
Their tunes inspired a happy smog.
With every leap, they made us grin,
As fireflies twinkled, we joined in.

So come, dear friend, let's take a stroll,
Through the grove, where laughter's the goal.
For in this place, both wild and free,
Even the trees hold a joke, you'll see!

Eves of the Eldest Trees

Beneath the shade of ancient boughs,
A raccoon held court, made funny vows.
He promised each nut a royal feast,
But left the lid off, oh what a beast!

The elder trees would softly sway,
Their branches tickled, come what may.
They shared old jokes, some sweet, some dry,
Like how the pinecones tried to fly.

An acorn fell with quite a plunk,
Landing in a porcupine's trunk.
"Oh dear!" said he, "What have I found?
A pointy hat or a treasure mound?"

So gather 'round, both furry and bold,
For tales of echoes, in whispers told.
With the elders giggling at every jest,
You'll leave the grove feeling quite blessed!

Simmering Secrets of the Serene Swamp

In the swamp where the lily pads twirl,
A dragonfly spun, doing a whirl.
He boasted of speed, but slipped on a leaf,
And landed with a splat, to everyone's grief.

The turtles, slow, shared their old lore,
About a race, with a twist to the score.
"We may be slow, but here's the trick—
We're really fast at pranks, just take your pick!"

A bubble popped in the muddy ground,
As frogs laughed hard—what a silly sound!
They croaked sweet songs of gator fears,
And how they hid when they'd see the sneers.

So if you're down for a giggle or two,
Join the swamp where the laughter's true.
With secrets simmering, joy's on tap,
In this serene spot, you'll need a map!

Lullabies for the Leafy Nest

In the nest where the branches sway,
A bird sang softly at end of day.
Each note was sweet, but oh, so wrong,
She'd mix up tunes and sing them long.

The little chicks, with giggles and peeps,
Joined in the chorus, but lost their leaps.
They'd flap and tumble, "What a delight!",
As mother just chuckled, "Sleep tight, sleep tight."

The wind whispered secrets through the leaves,
As father flew by with tales up his sleeves.
From funny mishaps to nutty quests,
Each lullaby brought giggles to nests.

So nestle close, let your worries away,
As laughter floats by at the end of day.
With songs and smiles from trees that bless,
You'll drift to dreamland, all cozy, no stress!

www.ingramcontent.com/pod-product-compliance
Lightning Source LLC
Chambersburg PA
CBHW070329120526
44590CB00017B/2839